SMILE

with My Animal Friends

D1517592

SMILE

WITH MY ANIMAL FRIENDS

Illustrated Children's Poems
Friendship Series, Vol. 1

Written by Alexandra Vasiliu
Pictures by Andreea Dumez

Translation from Romanian by Bogdan Vasiliu

Stairway Books

Table of Contents

BOING-BOING, THE PLAYFUL FLEA

"What am I going to do
with Boing-Boing, the playful flea?"
the dog was wondering in his cage.
"When I try to catch him, he jumps *hop!*
either on my belly or on my tail!
And I scratch myself all day long
until my fur becomes all curly!"

A BUMBLEBEE'S SUMMER DAY

A bumblebee on a stem
rolls his eyes around,
inspecting the garden.

O, how much he likes
to sit and to hear
what the auntie little ant
or the mouse chum must say!

See, he forgot
the old lady winter,
the empty pantry
and the fur hats.

MARY, THE LITTLE GRANDMA DRAGONFLY

Nobody knows
how much Mary, the little grandma dragonfly,
loves to read fairy tales
to her sleepy grandchildren.

First, she dresses them in pajamas
and covers them
with blankets of flowers
of mint and lavender.

Then Mary puts on her glasses
and slowly
opens a big book,
right at the fairy tale
about the sun.

The little grandchildren
are patiently awaiting
that sweet
"Once upon a time"
to begin.

And the little grandma dragonfly
is so serene

that every evening
she is not afraid
of reading loudly.

Only she knows
the secret.
Only she knows
when sleep's magic moment
arrives.

And then, in a big hurry,
she kisses her grandchildren,
"Good night, my loved ones!"

THE MOSQUITO'S ADVENTURE

Today the mosquito
went out to buy shorts.
But by the little petunias
he ran into the bumblebee.

"How are you, brother?
Where are you going?"

"I'm going to buy sports gear
to easily fly.
When everybody sleeps like logs,
all I want is to steal a hearty meal
all summer long."

THE QUARREL

At noon, the chaffinch had a fight
with the chickadee.

For a principle, for a word,
nobody knows any detail anymore.

Just the blue jay says
that she saw
what the chaffinch did!
That, being slightly vain,
he wasn't too polite.
But he even got lost
in dangerous quotes!

And the chaffinch,
seeing how time was passing
and his buddy was still dwelling
in a lot of vain glory,
from his boot
pulled out his water gun
and *bang-bang!*
He fired it with envy
that soaked him like a crab
from the bottom of a lake.

THE LADYBUG'S JOY

All day long,
the ladybug is swinging
either on an apricot tree flower
or on a dream's branch
or on a wild rose leaf
or on a cherry tree branch.
She is very delighted
that the harsh winter hid
after blowing frost and cold,
and the joyful sun
showed up high in the sky.

THE TALKATIVE GOOSE

In the garden,
we have a goose.
All day long, she cries,
"Honk-honk-honk!
Honk-honk-honk!"
Lots of noise!

Even when she runs
to bathe
in the pond
by the house,
her little beak
can't stay silent,

and she keeps us up-to-date
with what she sees
and what she does.
"Honk-honk-honk!
Honk-honk-honk!"
No stop moments!

"O, what a talkative goose!
It would be good
for her
to work somewhere
where there is
a lot of talking!"
thinks the lazy tomcat,
with a yawn
so big
that he almost swallows
the entire garden.

THE BUNNY'S DREAM

"However small I am,"
thought the little bunny,
"all I dream of is rivers of milk
to make me mighty,
and to not fear anything,
and to be sweet when I am kissed."

MEOW, MY LITTLE TOMCAT

Meow, my little tomcat,
is as big as a tangerine.
All day long he wants sour cream,
little fish, and even milk,
and if he does not see them on the menu,
he is very unhappy.
He cries loudly in the garden,
"Meow! Meow!"

ROGER, THE DALMATIAN DOGGY

I kept asking myself
why Roger, the Dalmatian doggy,
has black spots
on his little fur.

Eventually,
he told me,
whispering into my ear,

"My dear friend,
one evening,
while my mother was washing me
in the little soapy bathtub,
I rushed
to go out
and play a bit more.

And I went out
in a big hurry,
covered in foam and mud.

Since then,
the spots got
so dry
that they never came out
when I washed.

But I am not sad
at all,
because all the children
recognize me
as soon as they see me.
They start crying out,
"*He's coming, he's coming,
the most playful doggy
in the world!*"

THE POLAR BEAR'S SECRET

My dear kids,
I know you are wondering
why my fur is
white like snow!
Well, to be good friends,
today I shall tell you my secret.

I am not a bear like
all the other bears.
I am the giant polar bear,
and I am very respected.
I am also praised
because my fur is white
and without a spot.

But nobody knows
that at the North Pole
I eat only ice cream
all the time
and therefore,
I am so handsome
and always merry.

THE LITTLE SHEEP'S
HAIR SALON

"How is it possible
that all the sheep
are so elegant?"
wondered loudly Lady Cluck.
"Look how curly their fur is!
Clipped, white, and nice!
I can't keep my eyes
from them.
O, I would like so much
to know their secret!"

Hearing her pain
and not wanting to see her sad,
the little rooster told her,
"My dear wife,
they are so elegant
because they go
to the little sheep's hair salon,
where they all have
a special hairdo
with *permanent* curls.
Therefore,
whenever you see them,
they are all
dressed up to the nines."

A SWING

The little boy crab
is very inventive.
While watching the beach,
he saw the children
playing in their swings.

He watched them all day long.
He laughed and dreamed
until he had to run
home
in the deep of the sea.

While on the way home,
a thought came to his mind!
"How about asking
the pretty neighbor octopus
to swing me
in her big and strong tentacles
like in a real swing?"

This is what
any naughty boy does!

ROSE, THE LADY SEA HORSE

The lady sea horse
is a wonderful host
in her little house,
in the greenish blue deep
of the Pacific Ocean.

Swinging slowly on her tail,
she will welcome you
as soon as
you knock at her door.

She invites you to sit
on coral armchairs.

She brings
colorful candies
and never-before-seen cakes.

And when you are thirsty,
hop!
she puts
a little stylish teapot
up on her head
and, moving slowly
from her tail,
swoosh!
swoosh!
she pours
flavorful
chamomile tea
in sweet seashells.

BUZZ, THE METEOROLOGIST COCKCHAFER

Before going to sleep,
the cockchafer, Buzz,
flaps his little wings
over blooming apple trees.
Plump like a pumpkin
and with a cotton cap,

he spreads the news
to the sister bees in the garden
that tomorrow
will also be sunny,
and a lot of joy and fun.

THE MOSQUITO'S LIFE

On a maple tree leaf,
a mosquito is sunbathing.
He has sunglasses
and a cap a little too big.
He is sipping dandelion juice,
and he is looking around the garden
through a spyglass.

He wants to know
who will give him
a rich lunch today!
Not with okra or pasta,
but with a mountain
of tasty steak!
He can't go to the turkey
anymore,

because for one year
he kept going to him
until the poor guy became upset.
Is he the only candidate?
O, boy,
tough is a mosquito's life!
Without a meal,
just a wanderer!

HOW THE HEDGEHOG SHOPS

Early in the morning,
the hedgehog went
to the apple orchard.

But you won't believe it!
He did not have any bag!
No, don't be amazed!
I will tell you his secret!

The hedgehog
is hardworking.
Every autumn,
he fills up
his little pantry
from the garden.

Pay attention
to what he does!

When he arrives
in the orchard,
slowly, slowly,
he climbs in the trees.

Patiently
he shakes
the richest branches.
Rustle!
Rustle!

Then he quickly climbs down.
Laughing
and whistling,
he rolls on the colorful carpet.

Content, step by step,
he goes back home,
with all his thorns
loaded with
soft and sweet provisions.

Dear Reader,

Did you enjoy my children's poems? Did you like the humorous illustrations?
If you did, I kindly ask you to tell your friends about this book and write a short review.
I appreciate that you are standing by me as a good friend. Thank you very much.

Alexandra Vasiliu

About the Author

Alexandra Vasiliu is originally from Bucharest, Romania.

After earning her PhD in philology from Bucharest University in 2010, she fulfilled one of her dreams by dedicating herself to literature.

Her wish is to share a fascinating world of love, harmony, and graciousness with her readers. She's written children's books in Romanian and English including *The King of Time: An Illustrated Fairy Tale* and *Poezii Mititele Pentru Cei Mai Dulci Copii* (Romanian edition).

She now lives in the Greater Boston area.

To learn more about her, you can visit her blog, www.alexandravasiliu.net,

follow her on Twitter at @Al_Vasiliu,

or find her on her Facebook pages:

www.facebook.com/AlexandraVasiliuWriter

and https://www.facebook.com/CartiRomanesti

About the Illustrator

Andreea Dumez also grew up in Bucharest.

She has been painting and drawing from a young age, and her earliest memories relate to having a pencil in her hand. Sometimes, her dancing fairies and heroes would go wandering on the walls of the house or inside her parents' day planners.

After graduating from the Fine Arts University and the Pharmacy Faculty in Bucharest, she continued her lifelong dream in the creative arts domain. Her illustrations invoke her childhood imagination and her professional artist experience.

She is currently living and working in New Hampshire, participating in art exhibits locally and in Boston.

You can find out more about her artwork on:

www.andreeadumez.com

Twitter: @AndreeaDumez

www.facebook.com/AndreeaDumezArtist

To my dear little boy - A.V.

To my lovely little nephew - A.D.

Smile with My Animal Friends. Illustrated Children's Poems
(**Friendship** Series, Vol. 1)
Written by Alexandra Vasiliu.
Translation from Romanian by Bogdan Vasiliu.
Cover Design by Andreea Dumez. 1st edition.
Belmont: Stairway Books, 2016.

ISBN-10: 0-9970089-5-4
ISBN-13: 978-0-9970089-5-1

Made in the USA
Middletown, DE
08 December 2017